Caught Snapping Photographs III

Keith Pepperell

Copyright © 2017 Keith Pepperell

All rights reserved.

ISBN-13: 978-1543104448

ISBN-10: 1543104444

DEDICATION

To my spawn Jack, Alex, and Lydia all of whom have taken a snap or two

ACKNOWLEDGMENTS

Lady Joan Pepperell

Sir Francis Pepperell

Sir Arthur (Don) MacDonald Fowler

Lady Audrey Fowler

All of whom loved photography and were jolly good at it too.

THE IMAGES

California Morning

Lion in Florence

Drinking Away The Blues

Fountain of Youth

Fountain of Youth II

Lincoln Avenue Porch

Donovan's Pub, Galena, Ohio

Donovan's Pub

Donovan's Pub

Music Room in Georgia

By the Pool in Georgia

Snapping Sipping

Lincoln Street House, Westerville, Ohio

Log Cabin, Ohio

Freshman Football, Westerville South HS

Night Game

Taking the Field

Game Time

Ohio River Paddle Boat

Lunch in the Park

The Homestead

Homestead II

Attack of the Beast

In the Pink

My Friend is Starving

Winter Wonderland

Twiggy

Sunset over St. Kitts

St. Kitts Sunset

The Young Muppet

Florence

River Arno, Florence

Cathedral Santa Maria del Fiore, Florence

Florence

Il Duomo di Firenze

A Candle for Lady Joan, Worcester Cathedral

Renaissance Door, Florence

Frog Pond, Westerville Oh.

California Hills

Street Art, Westerville, Oh.

Worcester Cathedral

Knight's Story, Worcester Cathedral

Sunset over Dominican Republic

Worcester Cathedral, Tomb of Prince Arthur

San Juan, Puerto Rico

San Juan, Puerto Rico

Fortuna

Kitchen Bitch Lemons

Something Fishy Here

Worcester Cathedral

My Pal Gnomby and his Shroom

Scotchie's Bar, Jamaica

St. Thomas, Virgin Islands

Santa Barbara, Ca. Mannequin

Old Timers in California

My Sitting Room I

My Sitting Room II

Westerville Oh, Park

Westerville, Oh.

Dominican Republic

Sab Juan, Puerto Rico

Give us this day.........

www.ingramcontent.com/pod-product-compliance
Lightning Source LLC
Chambersburg PA
CBHW051048180526
45172CB00002B/561